WORKING

MOTHERS

The Essential Guide

Need
– 2 –
Know

Denise Tyler

First published in Great Britain in 2006 by
Need2Know
Remus House
Coltsfoot Drive
Peterborough
PE2 9JX
Telephone 01733 898103
Fax 01733 313524
www.need2knowbooks.co.uk

Second Edition 2008

Need2Know is an imprint of Forward Press Ltd.
www.forwardpress.co.uk

SB ISBN 978-1-86144-048-8

Contents

Introduction

You've probably picked this book up hoping there will be a cut out and keep magic wand inside that you can merrily wave at your life to sort it out; buying you extra time in the day, producing self cleaning kids and a husband who's home at 4.30 wondering what to cook for dinner.

If you think a book can do that for you overnight, then I'm afraid you're going to be disappointed. But this book can help you look at your life and isolate things that need working on to help you get a better work-life balance. Wouldn't it be great just to feel a bit more in control of things? To get your work, home and personal lives a little bit more in tune?

Working mothers are constantly coming under fire in the media for one thing or another and it seems hardly a few months go by without yet another survey about how working mothers would give it all up and stay at home if they could. Well, sure, if money was no object, so would I! Though I doubt I'd sit still for long ...

But what these surveys and the media who report them fail to take into account is that the vast majority of women in the UK don't work because they want to, but because they have to. And no, it isn't easy. I have yet to meet a working mother who hasn't had something to say about the need to *juggle or struggle*.

If you've picked up this book then you're half way there. Obviously, you think there's room for improvement, no matter how small and with that in mind you will find lots of tips and hints from other working mothers in this book, some high flyers and some like you and me, just trying to get life to run a bit more smoothly.

We'll talk about work and why you're there, how you can make time work for you (not the other way around) and what you can do to get your families to help out so that you can have some time for yourself in amongst it all, and that's whether you're a single mum or with a partner.

So many women just carry on, day to day, in the hope that something will magically change when in fact they just need to communicate. Don't be afraid to talk to your employer about wanting to work more flexibly or from home every once in a while – there are laws now which mean they have to listen. Do you know what your rights are? Has your employer let you know? If not, you'll find them outlined here and a list of useful resources at the back of the book for you to carry on with your own research.

And don't be afraid to talk to your family and suggest changes. You never know, they may actually be willing and want to make changes if it makes things better for you.

A woman I interviewed recently for mother@work was in the early throes of setting up her own business, 'What I need', she said, after talking about the long hours she was putting in, 'is a wife'. And she's right there, many women still fulfil the extra, unrecognised roles of mother and housekeeper, taxi driver and cook, as well as their so called real jobs outside of the home. No wonder the work life balance gets out of kilter.

So, if you want to get some of your life back, then here's where you start asking yourself some hard questions and making some even harder decisions.

Chapter One

Flexible Working and Time Off

Maternity leave - the April 2007 changes

The laws with regard to maternity and paternity leave and pay changed in October 2006 and came into force for babies born on or after April 1st 2007.

In a nutshell, as an employee you now have the right to 26 weeks of 'Ordinary Maternity Leave' and 26 weeks unpaid 'Additional Maternity Leave' - making one year in total (52 weeks). Provided you meet certain notification requirements, you can take this no matter how long you've been with your employer, how many hours you work or how much you're paid.

It's worth bearing in mind that your employer may have their own scheme which could be more generous than the statutory scheme. Check your contract of employment or staff handbook for details or ask your employer. Remember, your employer can't offer you less than the statutory scheme.

When your maternity leave is coming to an end, the notice you must give if you want to change your date of return from maternity leave has been increased from 28 days to eight weeks.

Optional keeping in touch days have been introduced enabling a woman to work for up to 10 days during her maternity leave period. Previously, going back to work even for one day would have made your maternity pay void from that day on – the keep in touch days are a way to allow you to do just that without affecting your maternity pay. However, these are not obligatory and it's best to work out with your employers when you will use those, if at all.

If you're uncertain about your rights, visit the DirectGov website for details of helplines at http://www.direct.gov.uk/en/Parents/Workingparents/DG_10029285

Paternity leave has also been changed and we deal with that in Chapter 8.

Dare you ask to work flexibly?

Many employers are coming round to realising that becoming a mother doesn't make you unemployable. You may have more specific needs than you had before, but companies are waking up to the fact that if they lose you because of their own inflexibility, they lose a valuable member of the workforce.

It's not cheap to replace and train an employee, whereas showing a bit of understanding where an employee is concerned can lead to a happier, more dedicated worker in the long run.

Many women, however, are afraid to rock the boat and struggle on working regular office hours when it doesn't fit with school or nursery care, leaving them tired and stressed trying to make everything happen to suit everyone else. *You don't have to do that!*

The government introduced flexible working laws in April 2003 to help protect both the employer and the employee by giving them both a structured system that the employee can use to apply to work flexibly.

This is a system specifically designed with working parents in mind and who knows, in the near future when paternity leave and father's rights are on the political agenda again, men might also use it more in order to help out more at home. Well, it's a thought! There's more on this in Chapter 8, The Role of Fathers.

It's important to note that these regulations are being reviewed and added to and it is a good idea to double check with the Department of Trade and Industry (DTI) website at http://www.berr.gov.uk/employment/employment-legislation/ employment-guidance/page35663.html as revisions may have been made since this book was published.

What the law currently says about flexible working

As of 6 April 2003 parents of children aged under six or of disabled children aged under 18 have the right to apply to work flexibly providing they have the qualifying length of service (at least 26 weeks at the date the application is made).

From 6 April 2007, you also have the statutory right to apply for flexible working if you are a carer who cares, or expects to be caring, for a spouse, partner, civil partner or relative who lives at the same address. This definition covers parents, parents-in-law, adult children, adopted adult children, siblings (including those who are in-laws), uncles, aunts, grandparents or step-relatives. Employers will have a statutory duty to consider your applications seriously.

The right enables mothers and fathers to request to work flexibly. It does not provide an *automatic* right to work flexibly as there will always be circumstances when the employer is unable to accommodate the employee's desired work pattern.

The right is designed to meet the needs of both parents and employers, especially small employers. It aims to facilitate discussion and encourage both the employee and the employer to consider flexible working patterns and to find a solution that suits them both.

It is wise to think carefully about your desired working pattern when making an application, for instance, will it mean a drop in salary? Discuss your ideas with other employees and present solutions to your employers before objections are raised – this will demonstrate your commitment to the company. In return, the employer is required to follow a specific procedure to ensure requests are considered seriously.

'Employers should sometimes have a bit more understanding. They should realise that you've got an employee who is more likely to work harder for you if you meet them half way.'

Paralympian Dame Tanni Grey Thompson

Who can apply?	What kind of changes can be applied for?
In order to make a request under flexible working guidelines an individual will:	**Eligible employees will be able to request:**

In order to make a request under flexible working guidelines an individual will:

- be an employee
- have a child under six, or under 18 in the case of a disabled child, or be the carer of an adult as defined on page 9
- have worked with their employer continuously for at least 26 weeks at the date the application is made
- make the application no later than two weeks before the child's sixth birthday or 18th birthday in the case of a disabled child
- have or expect to have responsibility for the child's upbringing
- be making the application to enable them to care for the child
- not be an agency worker
- not be a member of the armed forces
- not have made another application to work flexibly under the right during the past 12 months

be either:

- the child's mother, father, adopter, guardian or foster parent, or

Eligible employees will be able to request:

- a change to the hours they work
- a change to the times when they are required to work
- to work from home
- Working patterns may include:

Part-time working. For example, an employee might start work later and finish early in order to take care of children after school

Flexi-time. Employees may be required to work within essential periods, but outside 'core times' they often get flexibility in how they work their hours

Job-sharing. Typically, two employees share the work normally done by one employee

Working from home. New technology makes communication with office and customers possible by telephone, fax and email from home, car or other remote locations

Term-time working. An employee on a permanent contract takes paid or unpaid leave during school holidays

Who can apply?	What kind of changes can be applied for?
☙ married to or the partner of the child's mother, father, adopter, guardian or foster parent	**Staggered hours**. Employees in the same workplace have different start, finish and break times – often as a way of covering longer opening hours **Annual hours**. This is a system which calculates the hours an employee works over a whole year. The annual hours are usually split into 'set shifts' and 'reserve shifts' which are worked as the demand dictates **Compressed working hours.** Employees work their total agreed hours over fewer working days – for example, a five-day working week is compressed into four days **Shift-working.** Shift-work is widespread in industries which must run on a 24-hour cycle, such as newspaper production, utilities and hospital and emergency services.

How do you apply?

In summary, the procedure is as follows:

It is up to you as the employee to make a considered application in writing. You are only able to make one application a year under the right, and accepted applications will mean a *permanent* change to your own terms and conditions of employment unless you agree otherwise with your employer.

Within 28 days of receiving the request, your employer must arrange to meet with you. This provides you both with the opportunity to explore the proposed work pattern in depth, and to discuss how best it might be accommodated. It also provides an opportunity to consider other alternative working patterns should there be problems in accommodating the work pattern outlined in your application. You can, if you want, bring with you a colleague employed by the same employer as a companion.

Within 14 days after the date of this meeting the employer must write to you to either agree to a new work pattern and a start date; or to provide clear business grounds as to why the application cannot be accepted and the reason why the grounds apply in the circumstances, and set out the appeal procedure. In the majority of cases this will be the end of the matter.

If the timescales for the meetings don't work within your company, you can agree new ones but this must be recorded in writing by the employer and copied to you.

If it's 'no', what happens next?

The procedure provides an employee with the right to appeal against their employer's decision within 14 days of being notified of it. The appeal process is designed to be in keeping with the overall aim of the right of encouraging both employer and employee to reach a satisfactory outcome at the workplace.

In a minority of cases some employees will have grounds to pursue their request with third party involvement. This may be by referring their request to Acas (Advisory Conciliation and Arbitration Service), to an employment tribunal, or by using another form of dispute resolution. An employee is only able to take their claim to an employment tribunal in specific circumstances. In such cases, the employer must be able to demonstrate to the tribunal that they have followed the procedure correctly.

Time off for dependants

This always seems to be a vague, blurry area where no one is really sure of their rights. It's not uncommon for parents to call in sick themselves rather than admit they need time off to look after a sick child.

If you don't want to change your work pattern permanently, but you do have times when you need to take time off, then you need to know what your rights are here. It will also depend on your relationship with your employer and how they view this, as every employer is different. So it might be worth asking around to see what experiences other women have had in this situation so you get an idea of what to expect.

What is time off for dependants?

This is a right allowing employees to take a reasonable amount of time off work to deal with certain unexpected or sudden emergencies and to make any necessary longer term arrangements. The emergency must involve a dependant of the employee. An employee who uses this right is protected against dismissal or victimisation.

Is the time off paid?

The right does not include a legal entitlement to pay, so whether or not you will be paid is left to your employer's discretion, so make sure you check your contract to see what is says in there first.

Who is a dependant?

A dependant is the husband, wife, child or parent of the employee. It also includes someone who lives in the same household as the employee. For example, this could be a partner or an elderly aunt or grandparent who lives in the household. It does not include tenants or boarders living in the family home, or someone who lives in the household as an employee, such as a live-in housekeeper (should you be lucky enough to have one). This is currently under review and may be expanded to include people cared for outside of the home who are not relatives.

How much time is allowed?

The legislation for this doesn't actually specify a time length but it does state that 'For most cases, one or two days should be sufficient to deal with the problem'. For example, if a child falls ill with chickenpox, the leave should be enough to help the employee cope with the crisis – to deal with the immediate care of the child, visiting the doctor if necessary, and to make longer term care arrangements.

There is no limit to the amount of times this can happen, according to the legislation, but again it is worth pointing out that your employer can decide whether the reason you are taking the time off is justifiable and whether or not you are paid. It is worth making sure you deal with the problem quickly and efficiently, keeping them informed at all times and making sure you make up lost ground when you return. If your employer doesn't know what's going on, they will probably assume the worst.

What if my employer disciplines me?

If your employer decides you have taken too much time off in this way and decides to take action, you do have some comeback. Provided you can prove the time off was for genuine emergencies, then your complaint should normally be made within three months of the refusal to allow time off or from your dismissal (yes, it has happened).

If you decide to do this, you should go to a local Employment Service Jobcentre which will provide you with a copy of the booklet *How to apply to an employment tribunal.* This explains the procedure and gives the address of the employment tribunal office to which your completed form should be sent.

For a Pdf document by the DTI on time off, visit http://www.berr.gov.uk/files/file11419.pdf

Summing Up

You may decide once you have had a few years of juggling as a working mother that to get the ultimate in flexibility you want to work for yourself or start your own business. That's great if your skills lend themselves to that, and we'll talk about that later in the book.

But for a lot of women the option is to carry on working for other people and that can be very limiting.

However, with a bit of research you will see that there are many things designed to help you create a better work-life balance for yourself and your family – without your employer losing out.

It's worth asking your employer what sort of working system they would prefer you to adopt as you may find they have other staff working to a more flexible timeline that you could follow, and that avoids the rigmarole of form filling and meetings, which can be quite stressful.

But ultimately, stick to your guns, and get everything in writing!

Chapter Two

Time: An Alien Concept

So much to do, so little time

How you spend your time will have an impact on all the dynamics of your family – your relationship with your children, your partner and yourself. Their relationships with each other will also be affected so it makes sense to make sorting out your time management a family affair, wouldn't you say?

Isn't it down to me to organise everyone?

So many mothers assume the role of 'family hub' and when your babies are small, that makes sense. The likelihood is you're on maternity leave and in a better position to be at home and organising things.

But when you go back to work, whatever form that work takes, are you not entitled to a bit of help at home as well?

It's easy to carry on being the hub, even when you are back at work, and that means that in fact you are probably doing far more than you should be. If you have a partner or husband, then they need to realise that the kids and house are their responsibility too and that they need to chip in. If they are already chipping in to the family timetable then great – lucky you!

It's important though to make sure that what everyone is doing fits in with their timescales and other commitments, and you will need to be flexible at some point – if a teenager is coming up to exams then clearly, being hassled about their bedroom won't help.

Business management can help your home management

You might be surprised how transferable your work skills are into organising your family and vice versa. When it comes to organising some help for yourself in the home, you have to try and keep emotion out of it!

As Ros Jay says in her great book *Kids & Co*, you may feel like the kids get the better of you all the time, but you have one weapon they don't: all those business skills you already have that they know nothing about.

Ros Jay outlines using customer relations skills to make your family feel valued; selling skills to get your children to do whatever you want; negotiating skills to meet each other half way; motivation skills to generate enthusiasm in your children; management skills to get the best from your kids and teamwork skills to show your children how to get along together.

It may sound a bit draconian, but in fact it makes perfect sense. You've worked hard to become an effective worker and those skills needn't only be used at work. I'm not suggesting you turn your dining room into a boardroom or you operate your home from a desk in the spare room, but do take a few minutes to look at your workplace and see what might transfer to help you make time more efficient at home.

Does your company offer employee away days to help you bond and get to know each other better? Does your boss have regular round table meetings to get everyone's feedback and tell you what's going on? Does that make you feel included and part of a team? Maybe the same discussion and feedback would work regularly on a Thursday evening after homework with your kids round a shared meal.

One of the best and simplest tactics in the book to get everyone on side and more willing to help out is to treat them like customers. Even if you are stressed to the hilt at work, you'd never shout demands at a customer or client to get them to change their mind or buy a product.

'It's mainly a question of learning to let go. The first couple of weeks it was really hard not to control too much, some of it is just a bit of organisation and some of it is just complete chaos!'

Paralympian Dame Tanni Grey Thompson on the birth of daughter Carys

If you start off with a friendly tone and a smile, they're more likely to mirror you. The second you raise your voice or sound irritated, both customers and children mirror you. So to get what you want done quickly and efficiently at home as well, a smile and a confident voice will work wonders (and you'll feel better about yourself too). You'll save time and stress – a real win-win.

House like a bombsite? Getting the family on board

Clearly, one of the biggest bones of contention in any household is the housework. No matter how simple the task, it's generally met with a groan from the sofa – and that's just you!

The last thing you want to do when you get in from work is wash up, make tea, nag kids about homework, put the washer on etc etc. So, get organised. Call it delegation if you want, but just make sure that everyone knows what they are doing and when they are doing it.

If that means drawing up a rota, then do so, but make sure that everyone involved in putting the rota into practise is involved in setting it up. If they are involved from the beginning, they will feel that they are more part of a team than being told what to do.

Get everyone together (including your husband or partner) and talk about it. Find out when everyone has spare time around their work/school/club commitments and allocate tasks accordingly. Include even the smallest jobs or you'll find yourself doing them all the time.

Offer to teach your children how to cook, iron, use the washer etc so that it is initially an activity you do together and then they take over.

If it helps, incentivise the troops with a reward at the end of each week – it doesn't have to be anything big – a family size bag of popcorn to eat while watching TV on a Saturday evening or a trip to the swimming pool – something you will all enjoy as a reward for everyone's efforts to free up time for the whole family.

And do shake things up a bit from time to time – you wouldn't want to do the same chores day in day out – why should they?

'My daughter in law was so thrilled when she found that Sebastian could cook, clean, and sew on his own buttons. I got some things right.'

Shirley Conran on raising Sebastian and Jasper to pitch in at home

Once everyone gets into a routine, you will find that you have more time to spend together without you having to get on at people to do things all the time.

Buying in help

Most working households don't think they can afford the luxury of a cleaner, at least not on a regular basis, and some working mothers would simply not feel right with another person cleaning their house. They're supposed to have it all under control, right?

If you've been toying with the idea of hiring a cleaner but don't know where to start, then you could ask around among friends to see if anyone else has a cleaner that they would recommend.

Most privately hired cleaners will charge around £5 - £7 per hour, depending on what size your house is and what is required. Some charge separately for ironing and this is usually a lower rate of around £4 per hour. While there isn't a national average, the rates will vary somewhat from area to area and these rates generally apply.

If you do hire someone privately, it's still a good idea to have some sort of contract in place which you can easily do yourself. You can state if you want a notice period, how many hours they should do each week and can ensure it specifies if you have handed a set of keys over and when this was.

You should also check your household insurance policy to make sure it covers household breakages as somebody new in your house who doesn't know their way round may well inadvertently break something of value.

If you think having someone for a couple of hours a week is too much, then you might consider having a cleaner to do the big jobs once every couple of weeks, such as deep cleaning the kitchen or bathrooms, washing floors or windows, and doing the day to day superficial cleaning yourself. Time-wise (and psychologically), this is easier to manage and will be a distinct load off your mind, as well as being the best use of their time and money, leaving you with more of both.

The more businesslike way to hire a cleaner is through an agency. You may be asked to pay an administration fee that covers an initial assessment of your home and a monthly fee that covers all costs such as cleaning equipment. The cleaner's fee will be paid by the agency out of your monthly fee. Some also have a minimum term, eg six months, so you are contracted to pay the monthly fee, even if you decide not to have their services anymore.

In addition, as a rule, they will find you a replacement cleaner if you are not happy with the standards of the first or your regular cleaner is on holiday and they will also discuss any complaints you have with your cleaner if you want to avoid the discussion yourself.

Make time for you! You're no good to anyone burnt out

Remember when you had time to plan what to do with your time? When a weekend stretched ahead of you in a haze of relaxation and newspapers? Well I think we'd all agree that the lot of a working mother is a busy one, where the total extent of planning is what to have for tea!

But how many of us would also say that we just let it happen, that things hang together well enough and that in all honesty, you wouldn't go back. Quite a few, including me. I love the way our family works, we all pitch in to make sure everything everyone needs to do is more or less catered for, and that includes me.

And that is something we need to talk about – 'me time'. Yes, it may all hang together and yes, it may work for the family and your workplace, but have you remembered to put any time in there for you? Do you ever have half an hour just to sit with a cuppa and stare into space or take a refreshing walk in the fields or browse in a bookshop? Maybe, but when it happens is it planned or a happy accident? Thought so ...

'When the children were first born, I felt that the domestic side of things was all my responsibility but pretty soon I made the decision that work was more important than cleaning. I'm not Superwoman, so I organised a cleaner and delegated.'

Mandy Haberman, inventor of the Anywayup Cup

You're no good to anyone shattered, least of all yourself and your family, so if your idea of looking after yourself is a trip to the doctors, I'd say you need to be acting far sooner than that. (See Chapter 6 for more details on that.)

How do you make time for yourself? You plan it. Buy a handbag diary if you haven't got one already and put a line through 8pm – 10pm on Wednesdays and make sure that you do something you want to do. No distractions allowed – even if it is have a shower, lie on the bed, and read a book or call a friend you haven't spoken to in a while.

You might want to do an evening class, you might want to take up jogging but whatever it is, make sure the family knows that you are off duty during those hours. If it means making a meal for them beforehand, then so be it, but make sure you get that time completely to yourself.

To help this happen, try not to sit in a common area such as the lounge or the kitchen – bedrooms and bathrooms are far more personal spaces. And try not to let jobs creep in to this time – it is a time to rest, switch off and have a good think but *not to do chores.*

Isn't a 'To Do' list enough?

To do lists are a double edged sword. They are very useful as a reminder for things you meant to do but they can also start to become an extra conscience, sitting on your shoulder nagging you!

To do lists are OK at home if you keep them short and sweet. There's no point putting 'decorate bedroom' on a to do list as it may be months before you even get round to it.

If you do want to use a list, make sure it is a daily routine to prompt you rather than a taskmaster. And if you miss something, don't beat yourself up about it (unless it's 'pick the children up' or something equally important) just see if it's something you can still do or carry it over to the next day. It's your list, your time and you control both!

Summing Up

Your time is exactly that – yours. It may not always feel like it, but with careful planning you can make time work for you, not the other way round.

And don't forget to make time for yourself, don't just wait for it to happen. It's important for your own sense of well being. Involve your family in helping to run the house and their lives so that you all benefit from a bit more quality time – time you can spend together as a family.

Chapter Three

Childcare

Childcare is the biggest single headache most working mothers face. As well as the philosophical 'am I doing the right thing?' question, there's the 'who can look after the kids as well as me?' question.

Whatever age your children, knowing they are in safe hands while you work is the most reassuring thing and you will always wonder if you made the right choice so it's important to make as informed a decision as possible.

Broadly speaking, the most generally available forms of childcare are: nurseries, childminders, family members, nannies, before and after school clubs and workplace crèches.

There is financial help available from the Government and also from employers – see Chapter 5, Financial Help for Working Parents, for details.

Nurseries

Nurseries have been the subject of a controversial press in the last couple of years. One minute they're blamed for producing a nation of thugs, the next minute they're said to relieve levels of stress in children and the next minute we learn they are at the core of the Government's 'childcare for everyone' plans.

Nursery costs have also risen by 27% over the last five years, according to the Daycare Trust, which hasn't stopped them becoming one of the most popular forms of childcare after relatives.

The Government is planning to establish 3,500 children's centres by 2010 and use lottery funding to create 300,000 childcare places for pre-school children. They have spent £17 billion on childcare reform over nine years, with positive results. But it also needs to work with nurseries and other childcare providers to slow the number of childcare places lost each year and ensure that their planned free places don't undermine and jeopardise fee paying nurseries.

When to start looking

Finding a suitable nursery can take time and when you have, the chances are the waiting list will be long so make sure you start looking at least six months ahead of the time you will need the place from – even if you find yourself registering your bump!

Your local council or Children's Information Service (CIS) should have a list of all nurseries with contact details.

State nurseries are not allowed by law to take children until they are three and then it is for two and a half days a week, spread over five days each week. Some state nurseries do offer full days if you are both working, so it is important to check – don't ask, don't get!

Private nurseries offer a full day of care should you need it and often run late pick ups and early drop offs, though they may charge extra for this.

What to look for

Personal recommendation counts for a lot and you get the real picture, not the one the nursery wants you to see. If your friend's children are happy, then the chances are yours will be as well, though as with anything, keep a close eye on your child to make sure they are settling in OK.

The Daycare Trust recommends you trust your judgement and look for:

- Trained and experienced staff that respond to children's needs

- Busy but relaxed children who seem happy and purposeful

- Safe, clean and friendly premises and outside space

- Cultural sensitivity and a staff team and children who reflect local ethnic groups

- Fun activities planned for each day and a big welcome for you and your child

And that you ask:

- What is the ratio of children to carers? How many children do you care for?

- What qualifications/experience does the staff have?

- What are the daily routines? How will you involve my child?

- What are your discipline policies and how do you manage behaviour?

- Can I see a copy of your registration certificates and inspection reports?

You can also check with the Office for Standards in Education (Ofsted - www.ofsted.gov.uk) as nurseries now fall under their jurisdiction.

Nursery fees

In terms of costs, nurseries vary according to where they are; they are more expensive in inner city areas for instance. Generally speaking, a full week may cost from £200 upwards, and you may be eligible for help with these costs – see Chapter 5 for financial details.

Childminders

If your job means you work irregular hours and you need flexibility with your childcare that a structured day nursery wouldn't necessarily provide, then a childminder could be for you.

Childminders are self-employed carers based in their own homes and look after your children there. Childminders can offer a more personal and intimate caring relationship as they are limited to looking after a maximum of six children under eight years old (including their own) but only three of them can be aged under five. They are also allowed to look after children up to the age of 14. This does also mean that if you've got two children of different age groups or school levels, they can be looked after together.

'I think there should be nursery and pre-school places for all those parents who want it and at the moment it's the case where one in seven have places. I think the Government is full of relatively young men with young children and they understand these things. Or they're kicked into understanding them by their wives.'

Shirley Conran, OBE

Who checks the childminders?

Since Ofsted, the schools inspectorate, took over the monitoring of childcare two years ago, all childminders must be registered with them by law. Ofsted must also inspect childminders on an annual basis. These checks apply to both the home and the childminder. In addition, all childminders in the home are checked by the police (the Criminal Records Bureau).

If you're worried that these checks may not be stringent enough, you might be reassured to know that around three –fifths of the childminders who were assessed by Ofsted in the first round were failed at national standards. Why did they fail? Mainly due to breaches of premises or safety guidelines, such as kettles with dangling cords or gardens with unpruned roses – which are easily corrected.

Childminders who care only for children aged eight or over do not have to be registered or inspected by Ofsted and are not governed by national standards for childminding. However, like nannies, they can be approved under the Government's Childcare Approval Scheme (see opposite). Over-sevens childminders provide care before and after school, taking children to their after-school activities.

Is there a regulating body for childminders?

If you want to go a step further, you could ask for a childminder that is a member of the National Childminding Association (www.ncma.org.uk), a national association that has developed their own Quality Standards guidelines for good practise that all members must accept and follow.

They work in partnership with Government, local authorities and other childcare organisations to provide childminders with access to services, training, information and support to enable them to do a professional job. The childminder should be able to show you their up to date membership details.

Getting the relationship right

Communicating regularly about your child's development and behaviour, discussing any problems as soon as they arise, bringing and collecting your child on time and paying fees on time will help! Your childminder is providing a valuable service to you in their own home so don't forget to let them know it is appreciated.

Childminder fees

Childminders generally have an hourly charge which can vary from £3.00 to £6.50 per hour, with variations in-between for full and part time care.

Nannies - Mary Poppins or house invaders?

Having a nanny can be the most flexible way of working out your home and work life. If your nanny is live in, time pressures are not as strict and you know your children are safe in their own environment.

How do you choose a nanny?

Firstly, it is a good idea to check out what you can expect to know about your potential nanny. For instance, you can ask about a criminal record here or in the nanny's home country - as an employer, you have every right to ask.

Whether you do this direct or through an agency, be sure to actually take up the references - several court cases have been proven on the basis of previous employer evidence, so make sure you check with them so it doesn't get that far!

Help! I don't know where to start!

When average monthly wages can be as much as £1,400 for a live in nanny, you need to be sure you are employing a capable and trustworthy individual. An agency could be the answer.

There are several agencies that operate on a nationwide basis and there are bound to be some in your area that operate locally. It can be a very useful way to go about appointing a nanny as a lot of the legwork is taken away.

However, do ask what their routine is when selecting their nannies and remember you are entitled to see the results of the checks, not just be told about them.

Conversely, you will also be asked, usually during a visit to your home, to give details of yourselves, your children and your expectations. Any agency doing its job properly will tell you if you are being realistic or not and whether a nanny is actually the right solution.

You have to be realistic as to what you can expect to ask a nanny to do. Having the flexibility of someone at home so you can work late if you want to doesn't mean they have to empty the dishwasher and warm your slippers as well.

On a personal note, don't forget that you are inviting someone to be in your home for days at a time, perhaps permanently. Make sure you have the space, and the patience, to deal with that.

You may not feel as comfortable kicking your shoes off and flopping onto the sofa in front of your favourite soap if you have a relative stranger in the room!

How many children can a nanny look after?

Nannies usually look after the children of just one family in that family's home.

However in the case of nanny-shares the children of two or more families can be looked after. A nanny looking after children of more than two families must register with the Office for Standards in Education (Ofsted) as a childminder.

So what's an Au Pair then? Aren't they just cheap nannies?

Au pairs are single young people from other countries who stay with a family to help with children while they learn English. They can help you for up to five hours per day. Au pairs are not usually trained to work with children and therefore are not generally considered suitable to look after young children while parents are out. They can be a good option for providing after-school childcare.

Nanny fees

Employing a nanny means you become responsible not only for paying the nanny's wage or salary but also for deducting the tax and National Insurance contributions. The Inland Revenue operate an Employers Helpline on 08457 143143 for friendly advice on tax and National Insurance, or you could speak to an agency such as Nannytax (www.nannytax.co.uk) who do all that for you, for a fee.

Before and after school clubs

If your children are older, then a childminder may still be an option but you might also want to look at after school clubs. There are now increasing numbers of after school clubs - sometimes called Kids Clubs - in the UK. These are usually based on the school premises or in youth or community centres.

The advantage is that you know your child is safe, you know where they are, and that they haven't had to travel anywhere on their own or be collected by anyone else.

Some nurseries offer after school care too. A play worker may collect the children from school and take them to the after school club - some nurseries, however, expect parents to arrange this transport. The child is signed in and out when collected. The pick up time is usually between 5.30pm and 6pm and some offer breakfast club facilities from 8am for parents who need to start work before school hours. You would need to discuss this when choosing your nursery.

Before and after school club fees

Breakfast and after school clubs usually cost from £5-£9 for each session. Private after school club costs may differ.

Grandparents

If, like me, you have seen more of your parents since you've had children than you did for about 20 years previously, then it will come as no surprise that six out of 10 families use grandparents as child carers during the course of a year.

Each week a quarter of families with children under 15 use a grandparent to provide childcare (around 1,740,000 families) and where grandparents provide childcare they do so for an average of 15.9 hours per week. The Daycare Trust estimates that the value of this informal service is over £1 billion a year. That's quite a lot of charitable care being dished out!

While many older people enjoy caring for grandchildren, others may wish to, or may need to, continue formal employment, or may regard their later life as a time to pursue leisure interests or learning opportunities.

Also, as divorce rates soar, grandparents often are the main stabiliser in a family and the main point of refuge for children when things are difficult emotionally.

What are the rules for grandparents?

It's called 'informal' care because it's not considered to be a job of work, more a labour of love, but that doesn't mean you can't pay your parents expenses should you wish to, for food, petrol, money to take your children out and, of course, the care they give.

There are no financial breaks for grandparents helping out. However, there is a way round this. Grandparents can now be registered as childminders and get support and training in their role as a professional child carer, as well as being paid.

But, understandably, not all grandparents are willing and enthusiastic childminders. Some grandparents are still working and Age Concern is campaigning for the same flexible working rights for grandparents as parents and carers now get, so they can work and still offer support to their families.

There is also evidence to suggest that grandparents, particularly those with a partner who is unwell, find the childcare role difficult. Many find it hard to say no because they have an emotional investment in their families. So to ask them to become effectively regular carers could put them into a situation where they don't feel comfortable but are hardly likely to say no to their own children, ie you.

Lorraine Thomas, founder of the Parent Coaching Academy (www. theparentcoachingacademy.com), and author of *The 7-Day Parent Coach,* has come across this situation many times. Lorraine advises asking questions such as:

- How would you feel about looking after the children on a regular basis when I am at work? What would you enjoy most about it?

- What would be the most challenging aspects of it for you?

- How could I help to support you with those challenging bits?

- How much support would you feel able to give me - any time would be great (remember that you may need four days cover but Mum may only feel up to one - so make this easy for her to say).

If Mum says she can't manage for whatever reason, reassure her that this is fine with you and that it has no negative impact on your relationship with her or the children. Set up a probationary period so neither of you feels long term pressure. And remember to say thank you!

Summing Up

Make sure that you go with childcare you are happiest and most comfortable with, not just the closest provider to where you live. Trust your own instincts – you know your child better than anyone else, and it will help ease your mind to know that you have made an informed choice based on sensible questioning.

Chapter Four

Starting Your Own Business

According to the Office for National Statistics in 1997, 2.3 million of us did it; ten years on it's 3.2 million and rising. What is it? Working from home.

These are not all self-employed people; many are employees whose employers let them work from home all or most of the time, but nevertheless, improvements in remote communication have improved to such an extent that home working is no longer 'out of sight, out of mind'.

In fact, I was talking to a working mother at an event recently who set up her own successful import business at home and was campaigning to get people to say they were in fact *opting in* when they became self employed: opting in to a more flexible, controllable way of life.

What are the pros and cons?

Starting your own business can be a double-edged sword. Assuming you have taken the plunge and decided you've got the business idea to beat all others, consider these points:

Pros

- Flexibility – you can work your own hours, whether that's in the evenings after the kids are in bed or during school hours.

- Better work-life balance – having the flexibility means more opportunity to balance life against work.

- Freedom to breathe – without the constraints of layers of management above you, you can call your own shots and make them happen without the need for approval.

- Financial reward – at the end of the day, you own that company and once you have a net profit, that's yours.

Cons

- Flexibility – you are the person responsible and you are the one that will have to put the hours in – whatever that takes.

- Work-life balance – having to be 'on call' a lot of the time can have a negative impact on your work-life balance in the short term; it takes a lot of work to set up on your own.

- Freedom to breathe – you will be making all the decisions and acting on them, which can seem a very lonely and pressurised process sometimes.

- Financial reward – yes, a net profit is yours after tax but you are also taking all the risk, whether with your own money or the bank's. It's an incentive, but also a pressure.

- Loss of perks – you may find you start to miss perks such as pension schemes, holiday leave, sick pay – and someone to delegate to.

It's up to you whether you can see past the initial hard work to the benefits beyond!

Starting a business – is a franchise easier?

Many women are put off by the paperwork, mainly financial, that comes with setting up a business. But you don't have to shoulder that burden all alone.

Franchises often represent a safer bet as they are a tried and tested business model – you are buying someone else's proven idea and it is then up to you to make that idea work for you as well. It can, therefore, carry less risk.

'Now there is parental leave and maternity leave and things are better but you know you may lose your place in the ladder; whereas if you are your own boss you know you aren't going to so it really was very much easier for me.'

Prue Leith OBE on motherhood while running her own restaurant and cookery school

For the same reasons it is usually easier to get finance, as a market for the product or services will already have been demonstrated before and a recognisable brand established.

This means you should also have access to a business model and marketing plan. Most franchises offer these as a matter of course to get you started – a set up kit, if you like – and you should also be able to call on them for their advice and experience.

In some cases, a franchise will come with financial support as well.

And it doesn't have to be a grand affair; it can be something that one person can handle themselves or expand as they see fit, according to how business goes.

A franchise sounds good - what's the catch?!

While a franchise can reduce some of the risk, be careful. Some businesses that are up for sale may be experiencing difficulties. Make sure you fully understand the reasons for selling, as you may need to invest more money on top of the purchase price to make it a success.

You are going to have to pay money up front – that is your investment – so you won't make a profit until you have earned that money back (as with any business you invest in, franchise or otherwise).

There may be a set way to run the business which may or may not be a good thing, depending on whether you like to do things your way or not.

What's the nitty gritty of starting up alone?

If you think you've had the most amazing idea ever and want to go it alone or you've got the chance of becoming a consultant in your field, then great. But you have to do some serious homework before you hand in your notice!

And if you've been off work for a while and are itching to start your business up, be patient. You might be sure you've got a winner, and that level of enthusiasm and self belief is very important too, but there are some basics you need to check out first:

The market

- Who else does what you do?

- Where do they do it?

- Are they good at it?

- Is there enough of a customer base for you to have a share?

- As a start up, could you compete price-wise?

- How big are the others in your field?

- What makes your idea different?

- What evidence do you have that your products or services are needed?

- Have you talked to anyone else (that you trust) about it?

Be realistic with your business plan!

Once you've established all that, and if it still looks good (truthfully, not just in your own mind!), then you need to draw up a business plan. This is the document that will carry you through getting finance and it should contain as many in and outgoings as possible, even if it is loss making at first, to demonstrate you have thought candidly about your business idea.

If that sounds daunting, think of it like this: a business plan is just a map that describes how your business is going to succeed and what you need to do to ensure that it does succeed. Of course, if you are approaching potential investors you may well need more detail, in which case seek the help of a business advisor – Business Link can help for free (see Helplist for contact details).

However, if you're running your own business and you just want to manage it better, you don't have to go into that amount of detail. And because I believe that it is better to have any sort of plan rather than no plan at all, you can start with a two or three page plan and then develop it as you discover how useful it has become.

What goes into a business plan?

- A well presented cover – first impressions count!

- An executive summary – one page that sums up your business idea in a succinct, punchy way – you want them to be interested enough by this to read on.

- Table of contents to make it easy to refer backwards and forwards.

- A business description:

  An overview of your industry, a description of your products and services, details of who is involved and their backgrounds, a mission statement, an explanation of why you founded the business, details of the market you will reach.

- Your positioning - what makes you different and how you will market that.

- Your pricing – why you will charge what you will for your product or service.

- Cash flow statement:

  A cash flow statement shows readers of your business plan how much money you will need, when you will need it, and where the money will come from. In general terms, the cash flow statement looks at cash and sources of revenue minus expenses and capital requirements to derive a net cash flow figure. In layman's terms, what you make minus what you spend.

'I worked within the confines of being a mum and it became a lot easier when they went to secondary school. I would often work in the evening when they were in bed and at weekends. It was the only way I could do it.'

Mandy Haberman, inventor of the Anywayup Cup

A cash flow statement provides a glimpse of how much money a business has at any given time and when it is likely to need more cash. Analyse the results of the cash flow statement briefly and include this analysis in your business plan.

As with all financial documents, have your cash flow statement prepared or at least reviewed by a reputable accountant. It will save you a lot of effort and you will be able to work with accurate figures more easily.

Even as a self employed individual consultant, it is a good idea to have a business plan to refer to and check your progress against.

Working from home

Let's assume you have now done all of the above and are ready to start your business from home. Now the problem is, how do I make sure home stays home and work stays work? It's very easy to become obsessed with your own business and if you run it from home, the lure of the laptop can be irresistible.

Here's some tips to get you off on the right foot:

- Make one room the workroom. It may well double as home space too but only when you are not working there. Once inside that room, you are at work, not at home. Spouse and offspring knock before entering. Do not start tidying up, washing up or doing up your house – you wouldn't be able to do it if you were out at an office, don't do it just because you're there and you can.

- Make sure the converse also applies. Do not allow work to spill out into the rest of the home. If you need the dining table to, say, collate the pages of a big report, or pack some orders for postage then do it when nobody else is around and clear it away before they get back. It is your family's home too and you may alienate them increasingly by making more and more areas off limits to them.

- If you find it difficult to switch mentally from home to work attitude, dress for the occasion. No, not evening gowns and pearls but certainly office attire, including changing slippers for shoes, before going into your office and shutting the door. Then you are at work, physically and mentally. There may be nobody there apart from you, but you will think and feel differently and that will come across in your correspondence and phone calls.

- Keep strictly to your hours. Even if the hours you choose are not the ones an employer would have insisted upon, *write them down* and keep to them. Know at what time of day you expect yourself to start - perhaps a different time each day but a pre-set one - and on which days you work and which days you do not. Departures from that regime must have good reasons - business visits, holidays booked ahead, sickness etc. If the kids are noisy when they get in from school, knock off at 4.00pm and pick up again at 8pm for an hour – if you want or need to.

- If possible have a separate telephone number for incoming business calls - or a phone that tells you who is calling or gives a different ring for business and personal callers. You could even buy a mobile specifically for work – easier for billing and you know which calls to take. Then you can decide when to answer business calls and when not. A big problem once clients, customers, suppliers, advisors and the rest, know that you work from home is that they assume you are on duty until bedtime. Train them to realise otherwise.

- Similarly, make sure your friends know that just because you work from home it doesn't mean you are available for lunch/coffee/drop in chats/ shopping at all times. Of course, it is nice to do those things and you should schedule time for them (what's the point of flexibility if you can't use it every now and then) but make sure you stick to that schedule, and that friends know you are happy to see them, but is has to be planned.

Summing Up

Having your own business can be a liberating experience, but you are also never off duty. It can actually be harder to draw the line between work and family time, but you do have the luxury of being in control of your hours and ultimately, of reaping the benefits.

Think very carefully about what you are prepared to put into the business, including financially, but don't be put off by the risks that all business ventures carry. If you believe your idea or service is strong enough, then go for it.

Need2Know

Chapter Five

Financial Help for Working Parents

Are you running to stand still?

Many working mothers have gone back to work because they enjoy working and because they don't feel they are the stay at home type. But what they find is that the prohibitive cost of childcare means that everything they earn they pour straight into a large childcare piggy bank, leaving them with little, if anything, left over.

Many women complain of running to stand still in this respect and it can be pretty disheartening if your motivation is income. Some mothers actually find it better to stay at home or be on benefits than working and paying for childcare.

But this has been noted by the powers that be, and in the last couple of years several tax credits and benefits have been introduced that are for pretty much everyone regardless of income, in order to help parents, single or otherwise, back into work.

Some of the financial help listed below will be determined in some cases by your personal circumstances, so it is best to use this as a guideline and seek help from the contacts listed here and at the back of the book.

Medical benefits

During pregnancy and for 12 months after the birth of your child you are entitled to free dental care and free prescriptions – make the most of it! Your midwife or GP can give you the application form to fill in.

Statutory Maternity Pay (SMP)

You get SMP if:

- you have worked for the same employer for at least 26 weeks by the end of the qualifying week (the 15th week before the expected week of childbirth, which is approximately the 26th week of pregnancy) - ie you started the job before you got pregnant - and

- you are still in your job in this qualifying week (it doesn't matter if you are off work sick, or on holiday), and

- you actually receive £87 (before tax) per week in earnings, on average in the eight weeks (if you are paid weekly) or two months (if you are paid monthly) up to the last pay day before the end of the qualifying week.

How much is it?

For babies born on or after 1st April 2007, you should receive 90 per cent of your average weekly earnings with no upper limit for the first six weeks of your maternity leave. For the remaining 33 weeks the rate of pay is either 90 per cent of your average earnings, if this 90 per cent rate is less than £112.75 or if not, it is capped at £112.75.

The average is calculated from the pay you actually received in the eight weeks or two months up to the last pay day before the end of the qualifying week.

Your employer normally pays your SMP in the same way as your salary is paid. She/he deducts any tax and National Insurance contributions.

As a result of a judgement by the European Court of Justice, if your employer awards a pay rise which is effective at any time from the start of the set period used to work out your SMP and the end of your maternity leave, your employer must work out your SMP again and pay any balance due to you.

For babies due on or after 1 April 2007, SMP will start from any day you choose once you have stopped work to have your baby, which means your SMP will start from the first day of your maternity leave. If you have more than one job, you may be able to get SMP from each employer.

If your baby was born on or before 31 March 2007 your employer can't pay you SMP for any week you work for them after the start of your maternity leave, according to the law that applied then. However, if your baby was born on or after 1 April 2007 you may work for the employer paying you SMP for up to 10 days without losing SMP (Keep in touch days, as discussed on page 8).

Additional Maternity Leave (AML)

An additional 26 weeks of AML is available to women who have worked for their employer for 26 weeks, by the 15th week before their baby is due. AML is *unpaid* and begins as soon as ordinary maternity leave (during which you are paid your SMP, above) has finished.

Be aware, however, that your legal rights do change during AML. This means that your employer can suspend all other contractual rights and benefits, including pensions and paid holidays (although you may continue to receive statutory annual leave entitlement). So it is best to get a thorough understanding from your employer of how this will work before you take AML.

Statutory Paternity Pay (SPP)

Rights to paternity leave and pay were introduced in April 2003 and give eligible employees the right to take paid leave to care for the child or support the mother.

To qualify, you must have or expect to have responsibility for the child's upbringing, be the biological father of the child or the mother's husband or partner, and have worked continuously for your employer for 26 weeks, ending with the 15th week before the baby is due.

Eligible employees can choose to take either one week or two consecutive weeks paternity leave (not odd days).

The rate of SPP is the same as the standard rate of SMP - from April 2007, this is £112.75 a week or 90% of average weekly earnings if this is less than £112.75.

For more information on father's rights, see Chapter 8.

Working Tax Credit

Working Tax Credit is designed to help people on low incomes, whether they are employed or self-employed, and can include support for qualifying childcare. If you are reading this because you are planning to have children but don't consider yourself to be in a low income bracket at the moment, it's still worth reading on. If you decide to go back part time for instance, you may well find your income adjusts downwards so it's useful to know what you have available should this happen.

The extra help is available for people working 30 or more hours per week, disabled people, or people over 50 who recently returned to work after a period on benefit.

Working Tax Credit is paid via the payroll (though this may be changed to direct payment at some future point) and can be claimed by working persons who fulfil the required conditions. However the Working Tax Credit is not just restricted to those with children. The idea is to make work pay for non-parents as well. The following table gives a basic idea of who is eligible for what under the Working Tax Credit:

Working Tax Credit*	Amount
Basic element, payable to everyone eligible	£1,730 a year
Disability element	£2,310 a year
Lone parent / couple element	£1,700 a year
An element payable if you work (jointly) 30 or more hours per week	£705 a year
Severe disability element	£980 a year
50-plus element	£1,185 (if you're working between 16-29 hours per week); £1,770 (if you're working over 30 hours per week)
Childcare element (up to 80% of qualifying childcare costs)	£175 maximum eligible cost per week if you're paying for one child; £300 maximum eligible cost per week if you're paying for two or more children

*Tax year 2007/2008

To find out if you qualify, contact Working Tax Credit Helpline, open from 8am - 8pm seven days a week:

- Great Britain and Northern Ireland 0845 300 3900

HM Revenue & Customs (HMRC) will pay Working Tax Credit by Direct Payment to your bank, building society, Post Office account or National Savings account. If you're part of a couple or civil partnership and you both work at least 16 or 30 hours a week, you can decide who'll get the Working Tax Credit payments. HMRC pays the childcare element of Working Tax Credit directly to the main carer for all the children in the family, along with Child Tax Credit.

Child Tax Credit (CTC)

You don't have to be working to claim the CTC and the threshold up to which CTC can be claimed is far higher than Working Tax Credit (NB almost all seven million families in the UK are entitled to some form of this new credit). Households with gross income of up to £58,175 can claim (£66,350 for those with a child less than one year old).

It is worth up to 70% of eligible childcare costs of up to £300 a week for a family with two or more children, or £175 a week for a single-child family and that includes lone parents.

CTC is for people who are responsible for at least one child or qualifying young person. It's paid direct to the person who is mainly responsible for caring for the child or children.

The payment is made up of two elements:

- a family element paid to any family with at least one child and worth up to £545 (2007-2008 tax year)
- a child element paid for each child in the family and since the March 2007 Budget, is worth up to £1,845 (2007-2008 tax year)

You may get more if you care for a child under one or a disabled child.

In order to get the credit, a claim needs to be made via a claim form TC600. This may be obtained from the Inland Revenue or a claim may be made online via the Revenue website at www.inlandrevenue.gov.uk (Click on 'Child Tax Credit').

Without a claim, no credit is due. Furthermore, claims can only be backdated for a maximum of three months so don't hang around!

Child Benefit

Child Benefit is paid for each child you have, it is applicable to you if you are working or not, and is not means tested ie it doesn't take your income or savings into account. And it doesn't just apply to small children either.

You can claim if your child is aged 16 or under, and over 16 only if your child is aged under 19 and studying full-time up to A level, Advanced Vocational Certificate of Education (AVCE) or equivalent, or is aged 16 or 17 years old and has left school recently, and has registered for work or training with the Careers Service or Connexions Service (in Northern Ireland, Training and Employment Agency).

Also, you do not have to be the child's parent to get Child Benefit. You may get Child Benefit if you pay towards bringing up a child who does not live with you and no one else is claiming the benefit for them.

If you qualify, you will receive £18.10 a week for the eldest child and £12.10 a week for each additional child. Child Benefit can be paid into a bank, building society, Post Office card account or National Savings account that accepts Direct Payment and for tax purposes is not counted as income.

You can claim online here: http://www.hmrc.gov.uk/childbenefit/online.htm or by calling the following numbers:

- Great Britain Residents - Tel: 0845 302 1444/ Textphone: 0845 302 1474

- Northern Ireland Residents - Tel: 0845 603 2000/ Textphone: 0845 607 6078

Childcare Vouchers

On April 6th 2005 the government introduced new childcare voucher legislation. This allows both parents, (if they are employed and paying PAYE), to save Income Tax and National Insurance on registered or approved childcare costs of up to £55 a week and their employers around £370 a year in England, Wales, Scotland and Northern Ireland.

This means a significant tax and NI saving per parent of up to £962 per year for a 22% tax payer and £1195 per year for a 40% tax payer – not to be sniffed at!

The vouchers can be used for any form of childcare, from the ages of 0 - 16 years old, and can include, but is not limited to, nurseries, childminders, nannies, breakfast clubs, after school clubs and holiday clubs, providing the childcare is approved or registered.

To use this benefit, you have to ask your employer to purchase vouchers for you each month, up to the maximum allowed of £243. The company running the voucher scheme then provides the employer with the vouchers for its staff and all the necessary supporting paperwork. Several private companies run schemes for this, including many of the larger nursery chains.

This is a benefit designed to make childcare a more affordable, less prohibitive, cost for parents. By using the scheme employers can make continuing and returning to work a smoother and less costly experience for their employees, so it's worth suggesting it if your employer doesn't currently do this.

The direct cost of the scheme to the employer is between 4% and 7%, dependent on the level of service required. The total cost of vouchers and administration can be offset by the employer against Corporation Tax and the employer also saves up to 12.8% on their National Insurance Contributions when operated through a salary sacrifice scheme.

While this all sounds great, be careful! The Inland Revenue advise that using forms of employer supported childcare may effect tax credit entitlements and that parents should be aware that participating in salary sacrifice schemes could have an effect on earnings related benefits, such as state pensions and statutory maternity and paternity leave. Further information can be found on: www.inlandrevenue.gov.uk/childcare

Child Trust Fund (CTF)

Not strictly help for parents in the short term, but in the long term provides a nice little nest egg for the child concerned and therefore helps the parents out in the long term.

It works by giving all children born on or after 1st September 2002 a £250 voucher which the parents then have to open an account for. The account belongs to the child and can't be touched by them until they turn 18, so that children have some money behind them to start their adult life.

The CTF account offers you and your family and friends the chance to save up to £1,200 a year, tax-free, for your child. This is in addition to the contributions made by the Government - £250 at birth and, since the March 06 Budget, an additional £250 into the CTF accounts when the child reaches the age of seven. Children from lower income families will receive £500 in their accounts.

There have been issues with these accounts in that the administration of the vouchers has been dogged with problems, and even then parents haven't opened accounts to put the vouchers in when they receive them. If you don't open an account within a year, the Government will do it for you. Depending on the type of account they open for you, you may be charged to switch it at a later date so it's best to sort it out straightaway.

However, before parents or carers can receive the voucher, they must first claim and be awarded Child Benefit (see above).

Lone Parents

Lone parents who join the New Deal for Lone Parents may be eligible for some help with their childcare fees while they train or search for work. Information is available from www.newdeal.gov.uk or from Lone Parent Advisor's at Job Centres.

Summing Up

If you feel that it isn't worth you going back to work financially because of all the outlay for childcare etc, then make sure you find out all the things you may be eligible to claim for as it may be more than you think. Once you have established what is due to you and have set up a system for payment, it is very straightforward to maintain many of the credits and benefits listed here and it could make a difference to your monthly income.

Chapter Six

Your Health

Combating tiredness

Sleep - how it helps and how to get more of it

You need sleep to recharge your batteries, it's as simple as that. Without sleep you will not function at 100% and that will in turn affect all areas of your life, not least your mental and physical health.

Sometimes it is stress that keeps us going through each day. As energy levels are low due to tiredness, your body gets stuck in with a substitute (such as adrenalin) and that's why you can often feel 'frazzled'; your body is trying hard to make you feel energised against a wall of tiredness.

That's OK if it gets you through the day but when it comes to winding down and relaxing, hopefully going to sleep, you often find that your brain doesn't want to sleep. It starts to remember things you need to do and plan for the next day, you start to worry about family or work problems until you are wide awake again!

A simple way to stop worrying is to keep a notepad by the bed and write any worries down. Once they are written down, you don't have to worry about forgetting them and can comfortably sleep. In the morning you'll also be surprised how trivial some of those worries will seem. This works just as well during the day but don't let it become a huge list of 'To Do's' that weighs on your mind.

Sleep tips:

- Can't switch off? Lie on your back, arms by your side, palms upwards. Breathe through your nose. Now picture the air, really feel it, as it goes up one side of your nose and down the other. Comfortably slow your breathing and breathe more deeply so that your ribs expand. Alternate the sides of your nose for in and out on each breath, really concentrate on it. It's amazing how much this will clear your mind!

- Do not use the bed for non-sleep activities (sex allowed, if you've got time to have any), such as television, reading, studying, snacking, etc. Otherwise, the bed and bedroom become associated with wakefulness, not sleep.

- Avoid drinking coffee, smoking or eating heavy meals in the evenings as these can act as stimulants and keep you awake, though some people find that a milky drink (malt based is good) before bed works wonders – perhaps there is a comforting childhood association there!

- Make sure you have breaks during the day. Yes, I know that's hard to do, but even if it's a 10 minute break in the morning and 10 in the afternoon (preferably moving around in the fresh air) then your body doesn't have to unwind a non-stop day at night. See Chapter 2 on Time for some tips.

- Exercise! We'll talk about this in more detail in a minute, but if your body is naturally tired, your brain is more likely to follow suit.

- Restful bedroom - take a look at your sleeping environment itself. Is it cluttered? Have you got clothes piled up on chairs, shoes lying around, odd bits of furniture in the room that won't go anywhere else? If you have, sort them out, throw away what you don't need and buy some hangers. How do you expect to relax in an environment that is screaming out for your attention and valuable time? And if the clutter isn't yours, have a word with whoever it belongs to and establish a routine of tidiness that works for both of you.

But my children wake me up at night!

If your children are still babies, then your sleep pattern is pretty much out of your control! However, this is a huge area and I recommend looking at the parenting websites listed in the Helplist at the back of this book for advice on establishing a sleeping pattern.

That said, if you are having constant interrupted nights then the best thing you can do is go to bed early yourself for a few nights, even if it seems absurd to go to bed when your baby or toddler does at 7pm. It will help your body recuperate and you will be more able to cope the next day than if you had watched TV with a few glasses of wine (tempting as that always is) - you may feel relaxed at the time, but you'll feel worse the next day.

How do I get an energy boost?

If you feel tired at work or at home and need a boost to get you through the next couple of hours, instead of relying on caffeine or a trip to the vending machine for a fleeting burst of artificial energy, choose healthy foods to rev up your engine!

The right combination of carbohydrates, protein and fat eaten at regular intervals will help keep energy levels high. It makes sense to go for natural unprocessed foods as much as possible as these will actually keep you healthy, as well as giving you a boost. Fried or fatty foods can leave you feeling sluggish as your body has to divert energy to process it.

For a natural sugar boost, eat fruit and drink water with it. There is enough natural sugar in fruit to satisfy the sweet craving and the vitamins and minerals will give you a shot in the arm. If you don't want a fruit bowl on your desk, drink natural fruit juices, especially orange, to give your system a wake up call.

Not drinking enough liquids can cause you to feel fatigued due to dehydration, so make sure you keep a litre bottle of water on your desk. Aim to drink it in a day, or even better, make frequent trips to the water dispenser (extra exercise!) to keep yourself alert.

Your work environment

We're all now aware of the effects computers, air conditioning, fluorescent lighting, bad seating etc can have on our health, and a lot has been done to rectify these things in recent years. But you can still make sure that you help yourself by taking regular breaks from your work environment.

Even if you just go outside and walk round the building once or twice, you will feel fresher when you get back to your desk. If you can, keep a window open rather than rely on air conditioning, or even to combat over zealous heating in deep midwinter.

If you spend long periods of time at a desk, make sure your work chair is as ergonomic as you can make it by positioning it so your back is supported (many office chairs come with lumbar supports as standard) or by buying a cushion to change the shape to suit you. Ask a colleague to tell you if they catch you slumping in your chair – you'll soon start catching yourself! These things are the first steps to avoiding back pain and stiffness –one of the major causes of time off in the British workforce and is even more of a risk if your job involves handling or lifting heavy items.

If you really want to be a stickler for the work environment, visit the Health and Safety Executive at www.hse.gov.uk/index.htm, which also has a comprehensive section on New and Expectant Mothers.

Exercise!

Yes, it's the dreaded E-word. There's no way round it – to help stay healthy, you will have to get regular exercise of some sort or another. It will not only make you feel better and help you get more sleep, it will also help you get and maintain a more positive outlook.

There's nothing quite like the buzz after a good workout as those endorphins rush around you body waving flags and doing high kicks. You'll start to feel better and if you start to eat better with it, you may even start to look better too.

> 'One must learn to care for oneself first, so that one can then dare care for someone else. That's what it takes to make the caged bird sing.'
>
> Maya Angelou, I Know Why the Caged Bird Sings
>
> Bantam

Many gyms have now realised that people get as much benefit from a half hour class during the day as they do from an hour long class in the evening. As such, they have introduced impact workouts that are half hour classes you can fit into a lunch hour, depending on how close you are to the gym of course. Check your area to see what's on offer.

Yes, you're right, it is difficult to fit into the day and it does come down to good old willpower in the end (see Chapter 2 for making time for yourself). No one can do your exercise for you and there is no way to side step the fact that you need to move your body to exercise it. But that doesn't mean having to slog your way down to the gym every night; there are ways you can be more active day to day and in a more beneficial way long term.

Here are some quick tips:

- Take the stairs instead of the lift and if you are wearing flat shoes and feeling energetic try jogging up the stairs – if you do this a few times every day it will really help your cardiovascular fitness improve and you will feel a lot better and more energised for it. Chances are you've got stairs at home too so practise there as well!

- If you need to get some more water then walk to the water fountain or kitchen that is furthest away from your desk – even better if this means taking on a flight of stairs or two in the process.

- Get a pedometer (they're quite cheap and easy to use) and see if you are walking the recommended 10,000 steps a day. Put it on first thing in the morning before you leave the house and wear it right until the end of the day and just see how many steps you have done – is it 10,000?

- If you're not getting anywhere near that number think about how you could get more steps into your day even when you're working. The most obvious way is to walk to work and back if this is possible for you, and/or go power walking in your lunch hour. And that also counts if you're working from home –find an excuse to walk to the shops at lunchtime (need more fruit, for instance?) and really get some speed up. A gentle stroll is nice, but you need to get your pulse up for at least 20 minutes three times a week for it to be of benefit.

You can make this into a pleasant experience by going with a friend or colleague and use it as a chance to catch up on the news and gossip!

Toning at your desk, the kitchen table, on the train ...

There are some simple but effective exercises which can be done just sitting on your chair at your desk while you are working or on the phone. Some are 'invisible' so you'll be able to do them on the bus or train as well. You won't need any equipment, only yourself!

- **Buttock Squeeze**

  Sitting upright in your chair with your bottom pushed right back against the back of the chair, simply squeeze your buttocks together hard and hold for five seconds (remembering to breathe at the same time) then gently release. Repeat this 10 times holding each squeeze for five seconds. This exercise, if done several times during the day and every day of the week, will really help to tone up your bottom.

- **Tummy Tightener**

  Again, sitting nice and tall in your chair with your back straight and shoulders back, pull in your tummy towards your spine. Imagine someone has tied a piece of string to your belly button and is behind you pulling the string so that your belly button is pulled in towards your spine. Each time you pull your tummy in like this, hold it for 10 seconds, and make sure you breathe at the same time. Release your tummy and then repeat the same thing again another 10 times. This exercise, if repeated regularly, will really help to strengthen and tone your deep abdominal muscles and improve your core strength and posture (important for backs). The aim ultimately is to be able to hold your tummy in all the time so that it becomes something that you do subconsciously whilst sitting, walking and moving around generally!

Heel Lifts

Sitting in your desk chair with your back straight and feet flat on the floor, lift your heels slowly off the floor and then lower them down again. (If you have anything other than flat shoes on take your shoes off to get the full benefits of this exercise). Repeat this 15 times and you should start to feel your calf muscles working. To make this exercise more challenging you could place some files, books or reports across your thighs and then try the same thing. The added weight of these will make your calf muscles work harder as your heels have to lift against a greater resistance. Do two sets of 15 repetitions every day to help strengthen and tone your calf muscles.

Toe Lifts

Again, sitting in the same starting position at your desk chair as for the previous exercises, begin by having your feet flat on the floor (so also remove any heeled shoes for this exercise to work properly too). Keeping your heels on the floor lift your toes right up and then lower again. This works the opposite muscles to your calves, in the front of your lower legs. Repeat this 15 times, have a rest and then do another 15. If you do this every day at work, you will be improving the strength and tone of your lower legs.

Straight Leg Raise

Sitting very straight and upright at your desk chair with your lower back right up to the back of the chair, hands resting in your lap, sit with one leg out straight in front of you with your toes flexed up to the knee. Keeping the leg straight, lift it up a couple of inches and hold for five seconds then lower back to where you started. Repeat this 10 times and then change legs and do the same on the other side.

You will feel the muscles in the front of your thigh on the straight leg as you raise it up and hold it for five seconds. It is a good exercise for strengthening the front thigh muscles, especially if you do this every day at work. If, however, you have any kind of back pain then do not perform this exercise until it has completely disappeared.

'Health is not just the absence of sickness and being awake is not just the absence of sleep!'

Anon

Take a deep breath ...

It may sound too simple for words, but if things start to get on top of you and you can feel the stress building up, then take a minute just to shut your eyes and take 10 deep, wide breaths through your nose. You should feel the breath opening up your rib cage and expanding your abdomen. Ideally, you would want to find somewhere quiet to do this, so that you can fully concentrate on the breathing. There's no limit to how many times you do this exercise. The increase of oxygen to your muscles and nervous system really will refresh you and leave you feeling more calmer than reaching for a cup of coffee would.

Also, if you want to take it a step further, sit up straight with your hands relaxed in your lap. Hunch your shoulders up as far as they will go, again with your eyes closed if you want, and roll them backwards five times and forward five times. This acts as a massage on your mid-back and also helps loosen your neck muscles where a lot of tension can build.

Summing Up

To stay healthy and break the tiredness trap, you need to take action. Eat fresh fruit and veg, drink plenty of water, get out in the fresh air and get more exercise; just 20 minutes walking each day will make a big change. You'll notice the difference to your mental health and feel more able to cope with daily problems.

At the weekends encourage your family outside – you as well – to do something active; a long walk in the park/woods/fields, a cycle ride, swimming, skateboarding - whatever it takes to get those bodies moving. And as a family, you'll enjoy spending fun time together; putting a bit more life into work-life balance!

Chapter Seven

Staying Positive

With all that goes on in a working mother's life, it's easy to become stressed and many working mothers feel the day to day repetition of work and home gets them down mentally, to the point where relationships can be affected and they begin to think and act negatively.

Images of celebs and models coping marvellously, generally with wonderful figures as well as new babies, don't help our feelings of inadequacy – even though we know that 99% of the time these same people are probably less able to cope than us without their barrage of nannies, cooks, personal trainers, managers etc etc.

Even while knowing that you are making it all work, that you are juggling, not struggling, it is hard to stay positive sometimes and all it can take is for one small problem to appear to make you feel like the whole world is against you. You're not alone!

Exercise breeds positive thoughts

We all know that exercise and a positive attitude go more or less hand in hand, that one can feed the other. The exercise also helps with weight loss and leads to a better, more positive self image and self belief.

Taking steps – literally – to get yourself into better physical shape will have a great impact on the way you look at life and, more importantly, yourself. See Chapter 6 for more on Your Health.

Seeing change as positive

It is quite easy to be persuaded that change is a bad thing, that it is something to be scared of. Not so. Change can be the most liberating experience, especially if it is you making the changes.

Having a family will, almost inevitably, change the way you live and work. Whether that is as a result of your own change in attitudes to your life or a change of attitudes in the workplace towards you, it will happen.

Most of the women who get in touch with mother@work are looking for a way to deal with change – whether in the workplace or at home – but they have all made a positive step: *they have asked for help.*

You are not superwoman, nor can you twitch your nose and make everything OK all by yourself; you have to face up to change and deal with it and asking for help with that is a very sensible thing to do.

Talking to other people who have experienced the same things can help you deal with change in a positive way by helping you to understand it more. Change is unsettling, but as long as you retain some sort of control over it, concentrate on the end result, you can see it positively.

If the change you are faced with is definitely not positive – your employers move further away from your children's school or your childcare isn't working out for instance – then make your own changes to combat it. Have you considered asking to change to a more flexible working pattern to help accommodate school hours for instance?

The best way to make change positive is to make positive changes.

De-clutter your mental 'to do's'

Take a look at all of the things you do at home and at work. Are they all things that have a positive input to your life? While it is never possible to totally delete all the stressy bits from our lives, it is possible to narrow things down in many areas of your life to things that you either want or need in it.

Diana Wolfin in her excellent book *Back To Work, A Guide For Women Returners* uses a simple grid to help you prioritise your daily and 'bigger picture' life.

'Holidays? What are holidays? Holiday means doing something you enjoy. I enjoy doing what I do so I don't see me ever not working or public speaking or doing something with charities. I'd love to work with the UN; you've got to keep your hopes high and look up at the skies.'

Nighat Awan OBE, businesswoman and mother of three

What must I keep hold of?	What can I delegate?
What can I put on the back burner?	What can I jettison completely?

Fill in the boxes – honestly – and once you see on paper all the things that you really need or don't need at all, you will be able to start making positive changes to your life and feeling positive about the things you keep in it. It is not a question of weeding out what you can't cope with, but deciding what you do and don't want or need to do – taking positive control.

Keeping a sense of perspective

A sense of perspective might be the last thing you are aiming for when you've got kids to get ready, yourself to get ready, a mental checklist a mile long of things to do before, during and after work – and then you see the flat tyre. It can seem like dealing with one day at a time is all you can manage sometimes.

And that's fine, actually, if it gets you through *that* day, but don't make a habit of it or you will come to dread each day, not relish it. Perspective is all about knowing and remembering *why* you are doing what you are doing – the bigger picture. Perspective helps you deal with all the rigours of daily life because you know there is a bigger picture there. If you have set up a new business and it's created a hellish workload in the short term, just remember that in the long term you'll potentially be much better off and more in control of your life than before.

A sense of perspective can give you a more confident approach to life, as you will learn to worry less about the smaller things like housework because you know they are regular activities and simply part of that bigger picture. While thinking that won't make them go away, it will make it easier to take a deep breath – literally – and move on.

Maintaining positive relationships

Having a positive relationship with *yourself* is a primary need for a working mother. There is enough said in the press to make us feel negative about our choice (if we're lucky enough for it to be a choice), but if you are happy with being a working mother, then you are allowed to like yourself for doing it.

But if you genuinely question your own choice and feel negative about it, then maybe working motherhood isn't right for you. Unless it's a real financial consideration, don't force yourself into a situation that makes you resent yourself – this will only affect your relationship with the rest of your family. See Chapter 9, Guilt: The Final Frontier, for more on this.

Feeling positive about your choices in life will enhance your self belief and that in turn will affect your relationships with your family and friends in a positive light too. Only you can decide to be more positive, only you can make that positive change in your thinking, so do it!

Don't make the mistake of looking over your shoulder for how it might all go wrong or automatically focus on the mistakes you, or members of your family, made that day. Take time to see how things could go well for you, and each evening take time to think about something positive that's happened to you or them or that you have done well – it's amazing what the feel-good factor can be from simply reminding yourself that good stuff happens too.

Happy families?

When was the last time you greeted your children/husband/partner/dog with the words 'Hello darling/s, how wonderful to see you. Have you had a good day? Tell me about it!'. I'll bet it wasn't recently (if ever, to be fair) and if you did greet them now with that level of enthusiasm they'd be checking your breath for alcohol rather than taking it at face value.

But how much nicer it would be if instead of only communicating when you need them to eat/get dressed/do chores you took time out to talk to them in a social way. This is not something that will happen instantly or overnight. Chances are you have all become used to your daily pattern of grunts and demands as you all rush about in the mornings and evenings, but look for a time when you can suggest turning off the TV, X-Box, stereo, computer, mobile phone and actually sit down and play a game together or go to the pictures –whatever your family gathering of choice would be.

But they don't want to talk to me!

With older children, ie teenagers, it can often be the case when they want nothing more than to go to their rooms and stay there until hunger drives them to the kitchen. And one of the simplest ways to get everyone together is to have a family meal, even if it is just once a week on a Sunday, so that you are together and there is an opportunity to talk (or at least just be together). And to avoid rows, try making the conversation about anything other than your family issues eg a film, sports teams, music, friends.

You can even explain to your family why it is you want to instigate this. Make it a time when stories of the week are swapped, but try to keep it upbeat and focus on the positives that have happened, not the negatives.

It's always easy to focus on the negatives in a family as these are the things that tend to need dealing with, so that it can often be weeks before the whole family get together collectively to see how well things are going.

Kicking the negative thinking

We've just been talking about how you can make things a bit more positive at home but you also need to make sure that you are thinking positively about your own life. After all, if you think negatively about yourself and what you are doing, then that will get picked up on at home and it will pressurise those positive relationships you have built up.

'Be nice to someone, compliment their outfit at work or congratulate them on a good piece of homework. You'll feel good about making them feel good and if you get a compliment in return, you'll feel good too.'

'One kind word can warm three winter months'

Japanese proverb.

Be more assertive with yourself! If you think that you can't change the way things are and that 'it's not perfect but it muddles along OK' then you are doing yourself a great disservice. Try and talk to other positive people – if when you do see your friends you all have a good moan about your jobs, families or dress sizes over wine and pizza, that's fine once in a while. But try suggesting you steer clear of that subject sometimes (hard to do, I know!) and talk about other things like holiday planning, have a trip to the shops, suggest all going to the gym together, have a sponsored diet.

In short, your mood of positive thinking will be seriously hampered if you surround yourself with negative people who enjoy a good moan, but make no move to positively change things.

Improve your self-esteem

It is an easy trap to fall into when you are busy at work and home – you get tired, but you can't catch up, then you just carry on because you have to and suddenly, you start to criticise yourself for making little mistakes –because you are tired!

Your self esteem suffers because instead of changing your routine and making the most of your time (see Chapter 2) or giving yourself a health check (see Chapter 6) you just assume that you can't cope.

Maybe you can't, with the way things stand, but *there is no such thing as superwoman!* If you've only made two little mistakes in a week, then you're doing better than me. You are only human and it is up to you to make changes and to choose what you do, or don't do.

Summing Up

In the same way as you reminded yourself earlier about all the reasons you do what you do in order to give yourself a sense of perspective, you need to remind yourself how much you achieve each day. Try not to worry about the small stuff that goes wrong – we all drop the ball sometimes.

Running a family, a home and a job is actually *three jobs,* requiring flexibility, versatility, management skills, negotiation skills, supreme organisational skills, administrative excellence, financial management and the patience of a saint, not to mention the domestic skills of Mrs Beeton – so cut yourself some slack!

Chapter Eight

The Role of Fathers

We all know that families are a two-parent thing, right? Well, no, not exactly. For a start, more than a third of children are being brought up by single parents now and with the culture we have developed in the UK, we work longer hours than most other European countries. This means that it is generally one parent who takes on the bulk of the childcare and it is generally the mother that takes this task on.

In recent years, plans have been made to start shifting the balance for those fathers who would genuinely like to spend more time with their families without it having a stigma attached to it. There are national organisations such as Fathers Direct that are designed to help fathers break away from the traditional view of absent commuter and which are also having a greater public say in how employer attitudes should be changing.

So what's been done so far?

Paternity leave legislation is a big first step as it recognises the need for involvement of the father in a child's life right from the beginning, and as of October 2005 hundreds of thousands of new fathers were given a boost when the government confirmed plans to give them up to *three months* paid paternity leave.

There is, however, stiff opposition to this from trade and industry bodies, so it will not happen without a struggle.

If employers don't like it, what can they do?

Although the pay gap is shortening, it is far from being equal. This means that men are still more or less the main breadwinners in most families and when children are born, the need for a stable income increases and, as we know, never really goes away.

It is only very recently that more men have begun to go against the grain and take what some see as a risk by requesting flexible working or time off with the family. Work culture in this country demands 200% commitment and with unemployment being what it is, competition for good jobs is fierce.

In fact, research by the Daycare Trust into the father's role found that 8 out of 10 fathers complained that hectic work schedules created difficulties fulfilling family duties and household tasks, but felt forced into longer hours to provide for their children.

However, just as women are protected by law when going back to work or leaving on maternity leave, so men are too. Employees are protected from suffering unfair treatment or dismissal for taking, or seeking to take, paternity leave. Employees are also entitled to return to the same job following paternity leave, and those who believe they have been treated unfairly can complain to an employment tribunal.

How much time can be taken on paternity leave?

Initial rights to paternity leave and pay were introduced in April 2003 along with the flexible working regulations (see Chapter 1) and it provides a much needed support mechanism for mothers after the birth of a child. Up to two weeks can be taken by the father, which must be taken within 56 days after the birth of the child.

If that doesn't seem like enough, the fact that an employee continues to accrue annual leave while on paternity leave should help. In theory, even if he has no rights to annual leave under his contract of employment, he will be entitled to the equivalent of four weeks paid annual leave under the Working Time Regulations 1998. This may not be automatic as an employer is also entitled to use an accrual system where holiday builds over a period of time, but it is worth looking into to see if he is eligible. See the DTI webpage for the latest information on this: http://www.berr.gov.uk/employment/workandfamilies/paternity-leave/index.html.

Can he take holiday as well without getting into trouble at work?

It's also worth noting that although an employee isn't entitled to take annual leave *during* paternity leave, ie in the middle of the two weeks, subject to the usual arrangements with his employer, there is no reason why he cannot take a period of annual leave immediately before or after paternity leave.

This means that in theory, a father could have up to six weeks at home if he chose to take his four weeks contractual annual leave on top of two weeks paternity leave.

Of course, all this is subject to discussions with employers and you might prefer to save up holiday for when the baby is a bit older. But do look into it as fathers who do want to have time off with their children may not realise they have these options.

Statutory Paternity Pay (SPP)

During their paternity leave, most employees are entitled to Statutory Paternity Pay from their employers.

SPP is paid by employers for either one or two consecutive weeks as the employee has chosen. The rate of SPP is the same as the standard rate of SMP - from April 2007, this is £112.75 a week or 90% of average weekly earnings if this is less than £112.75.

Employees who have average weekly earnings below the Lower Earnings Limit for National Insurance purposes (£87 a week from April 2007) do not qualify for SPP. Employees who do not qualify for SPP, or who are normally low-paid, may be able to get Income Support while on paternity leave.

Additional financial support may be available through Housing Benefit, Council Tax Benefit, Tax Credits or a Sure Start Maternity Grant. Further information is available from your local Jobcentre Plus office or Social Security office.

'Once men start asking how can we juggle work and family the way that women have always done, then we begin to crack the problem.'

Jenni Murray, Radio 4's Woman's Hour presenter

Note: the figures quoted in this chapter for rates of SPP and the lower earnings limit are correct at the time of going to press. Your local Inland Revenue office can advise you of the current rates.

Is there somewhere I can find out more?

There are now several organisations that have been set up to provide practical and emotional support to fathers. Unfortunately, the more radical aspects of this, such as the now disbanded Fathers4Justice, have muddied the waters somewhat by their publicity seeking stunts in fancy dress (remember Batman at Buckingham Palace?), but you shouldn't let this deter you!

Fathers Direct

Fathers Direct is 'the national information centre on fatherhood' and you can find it at www.fathersdirect.com. Since their inception in 1999, Fathers Direct has rapidly become an influential organisation regularly consulted on policies and often quoted in the media. They help Government, employers, services for families and children, and families themselves to adapt to changing social roles of men and women.

There's loads of advice and information on there, covering a multitude of issues, so if your husband/partner needs a reassuring starting point, then this is it.

For Parents by Parents

Lots of advice, personal experiences, and information on everything from finance and legal issues to work issues and personal issues such as post natal depression in men, single fatherhood and changes in relationships after children. www.forparentsbyparents.com/dad.html

HomeDad.org.uk

Recent research indicates that there are now 200,000 men staying at home to look after the home and family in the UK. And not just house-husbands at home full-time but increasing numbers of fathers who are working part-time and sharing the childcare, or bringing up children by themselves.

A well thought out site that provides plenty of personal information from it's members and takes a big step to demystifying why men might want to stay at home too. Find it at www.homedad.org.uk/index.html

Summing Up

It seems there is a genuine wind of change blowing through attitudes to fatherhood at the moment and although it may not make a big difference to the current generation of working mothers, it will make a big difference to our sons and daughters. Start by supporting the organisations talked about here and by setting an example in your own family.

Chapter Nine

Guilt: The Final Frontier

What does every working mother have in common? Clue: you feel it when you go back to work and you feel it when you stay at home – *guilt*.

It's a horrible emotion and it can make you irritable, irrational, and frankly, a misery! But it's not something to be ashamed of, in fact, it would take someone who was extremely sorted emotionally to be able to deny any guilt at all. But it is possible to minimise the guilt and deal with it head on.

As a mother, you are programmed to put your children first. It's in your genes, a throw back to the days when mothers instinctively protected their children against predators. Now the predators are gone, but still we persist in feeling that we are the only people in the world who know what's best for our children and that makes us feel guilty whenever we have a thought about our own careers or even time alone!

'Working mothers like me are used to being made to feel guilty. If they still burned witches at the stake, the first in line for the bonfire would be those who handed over their children to someone else so they could stir their cauldrons full-time.' So says Lowri Turner. Well, that's one woman's view and I bet there are quite a few who share it!

But what does guilt feel like?

It can be like a feeling of shame, without perhaps even knowing exactly what we feel bad about. There is such a thing as real guilt. We have a built in system - 'conscience' - which tells us when we are doing something wrong. With real guilt, we will feel guilty about particular things, and it is a good indicator that perhaps things need to change.

It's also highly likely that with a tight routine of children and work to organise day in, day out, you are feeling stressed to some degree and this affects your emotions in a negative way anyway. Stress will exacerbate any feelings of guilt you are having so you must take that into account when assessing your guilt levels.

Does guilt mean I'm wrong?

Not necessarily! Guilt is a good indication that you might not have things balanced the way you'd like, but you'll never get rid of guilt entirely. As a normal human being, you are likely to feel that you don't want to let anyone down and by not being at work or not with your family, you may feel you are letting them down. Letting them down = guilty feelings. This is where getting a better balance comes in.

Even icons like Madonna, for all their wealth and army of nannies, admit they find getting the balance right hard work. Sobbing into the camera, Madonna said in her documentary, *I'm Going To Tell You A Secret*, 'One day you will know the polarity of work and family and the struggle to keep it all balanced.' If she can't manage it, what hope have you got? So don't feel bad about guilt, it's a human thing and a necessary thing that, if anything, shows you that you care a lot – and that's not a bad thing!

Who is making you feel guilty?

'Silly question, me of course!' you might say. And yes, to a point you are your own worst enemy by allowing guilt to take over. But what is it that triggers the guilt? Why do you feel guilty at dropping your kids off at childcare?

You are entitled to carry on with your own life even though you are now a mother! There, I've said it. OK, it might be a very different kind of life and you will inevitably have a period of adaptation and acceptance of that, but don't feel that you are *wrong* for wanting to have a life after children.

Society is different now. Only 30 or 40 years ago it wasn't accepted that women with children should work as well. Don't forget, the equal pay act was only introduced 30 years ago and we still haven't managed to get pay fully

'There are companies that are much more sympathetic to working mums and women should seek them out. If you feel guilty every time you take time out to go to the school concert or take your child to the doctor, it is not the way to live.'

Prue Leith, OBE

equal yet! If you got married back then, often that was enough for you to have to leave work to look after the household, let alone when you had children. There was no question about who would run the house and look after the children. These issues are still around in older generations today and knowing that your own parents or grandparents *may* think you are wrong is also a route to feeling *disapproved* of and therefore guilty.

So try not to feel guilty about wanting to eventually get on with your life!

Make your own mind up

Let's face it, there isn't a month goes by that someone somewhere hasn't produced a survey that tells us how bad we are as working mothers to 'dump' our children, or on the flip side to tell us how we shouldn't be wasting our skills and education and get back to work.

But in reality, all these surveys are about different women all over the country in different situations. It is really impossible to generalise and, after all, you know you the best. It is up to you to decide that you have made the best decisions you could at the time and that you are going to make it work. Don't let doubt, and inevitably guilt, change that or you may well resent it later on.

Equally, some women know in their heart of hearts that they really want to be with their family full time and that's great – they've also listened to their guilt and it's told them what they needed to know. Don't be afraid to look your guilt in the eye and make changes if that's what is needed.

Take an honest look at yourself!

So how do we deal with this? There is no one answer that will make your guilt go away, and it's important to realise that it is a process, not an instant thing (since when were human emotions that easy to tame?).

Start by being honest with yourself. Write down a list of the reasons why you went back to work initially or why you want to go back to work. Then write a list of reasons why you work now or not. Try and list both positives and negatives – it's too easy to focus just on the problems.

When you look at the lists, are the reasons you work now still the same as the reasons you went back to work for originally? Is the only reason you're going back to work for the money? Are you actually happy at home but feeling pressure from elsewhere to go back to work? If the two lists are very different, think about how they are and whether you are happy with that. What's in those lists that makes you feel uneasy about them?

If the problem is work

One of the main routes for feeling guilty about working is because you're not enjoying it or it isn't satisfying anymore. You wonder why you're doing this job when you could be having more fun with your kids. If one of the main reasons you went to work is because you felt fulfilled when you worked but you aren't now, then in fact it may be your job you need to be looking at, not your lifestyle.

It may be that you simply need a change of work scenery to rejuvenate your interest and satisfaction levels.

If the reason you work is because you need the money but you aren't happy in your job, then look at finding a new job or re-training. Learning new skills can be a huge confidence boost and will give you a new lease of enthusiasm for your job or even give you the opportunity to change roles within the company you are with.

Of course, finding a new job when you have children can be a challenge in its own right and is the reason many women rise to the challenge of starting their own business or becoming consultants – more about this in Chapter 4.

Take a look at your children – happy or sad?

Are your children happy? Do you feel guilty because you're not there when they get in from school or because they go to a childminder? Have you actually asked them what they think of all this?

Children can be brutally honest and also petulant and stroppy. But then so can parents! If you have simply told them that this is what's happening and they have to get on with it, they are going to feel dictated to. If you discuss it with them, ask how they feel or if they have any ideas about how to make the whole thing hang together, then you might be surprised at the response you get.

They will, after all, have their own ideas and will also know what other parents do and don't do. Equally, children can be very adept at pushing the right emotional buttons to make the most of your guilt so try to make sure you stay objective and factual in your discussions with them!

Do they know why you do what you do?

If you're feeling guilty about working, then it might be time to explain to your family why you work. If you work because your wage pays for all the after school activities and clubs they go to, then let them know that.

Does the money make it all worthwhile?

The million-dollar question. Many of us work because we are maintaining a lifestyle we had before our children were born. Women are waiting until they are older to have children, the likelihood is they will have their own flat or house, car, are used to holidays etc and have followed a career. Once you have children, if you want all of that to continue, with or without a partner, then it has to be paid for.

So consider this - if you are feeling guilty because you're spending a lot of time in the office and not with your kids but you have a nice car, ask yourself which is more important? Keeping up appearances or keeping a relationship with your kids? I'm not suggesting you go and run an organic farm in Dorset, but many people are realising the realities of the smoke and mirrors of our spend heavy society and it's true – you really can't take it with you.

'All working mothers feel guilt. Working women don't tend to feel guilt, only working mothers. The second you feel guilt, say 'does my partner feel guilt?'. Then you'll be rolling around on the floor laughing merrily at the very idea.'
Shirley Conran OBE

Helplist

Financial

Child Benefit
www.inlandrevenue.gov.uk/childbenefit/
Telephone: 0845 302 1444
Textphone: 0845 302 1474
Northern Ireland 0845 603 2000

Working Tax Credit/Child Tax Credit Helpline
Open from 8am - 8pm seven days a week
In Great Britain 0845 300 3900 (textphone 0845 300 3909)
From outside the UK +44 135 535 9007

Entitled To
www.entitledto.co.uk
A website that has calculators on it so you can instantly find out if you would
be eligible for something or not.

Independant Financial Advisors (IFA)
www.unbiased.co.uk
Business Hotline: 0800 085 3251
Consumer Hotline: 0800 085 3250
For details of an IFA in your area to give you an unbiased overview of your
financial needs.

Moneyfacts
www.moneyfacts.co.uk
Independent and impartial personal finance website. Provides interest rates on
all types of bank & building societies' accounts, mortgages, credit cards and
personal loans throughout the UK.

Directgov

www.direct.gov.uk/Homepage/fs/en

All your legal rights explained on this government website, including which benefits and credits are available to whom.

Bank of Scotland

www.bankofscotland.co.uk/corporate/index.html

One of the first and only banks to have a comprehensive and dedicated Women In Business unit that drives a unique programme throughout the UK.

Flexible Working / Time Off for Dependants

mother@work

www.motheratwork.co.uk

mother@work deals with working lives, family lives and personal lives, with practical advice and information to help you get the balance right.

Working Families

www.workingfamilies.org.uk

Free Helpline: 0800 013 0313

Charity working to help children, working parents, and carers and their employers find a better balance between responsibilities at home and work. Advice given on maternity and paternity leave, rights at work, tax credits and benefits, and support to negotiate friendly family hours. Free factsheets and an online guide to flexible working can be found on the website.

ACAS

www.acas.org.uk

Mediating in employment; advice on good industrial relations practice, including equal pay.

Employers and Work-Life Balance

www.employersforwork-lifebalance.org.uk

Tel: 020 7976 3500

Run by The Work Foundation, EaWLB aims to help all UK organisations implement and continuously improve sustainable work-life strategies which meet customer needs, corporate goals and enhance the quality of life for individuals.

Childcare

Childcare Link

www.childcarelink.gov.uk

Freefone: 08002 346 346

Helps you find useful information about the different types of childcare and early education in your local area. The site also contains details of your local Children's Information Service, who can provide additional help and advice with all aspects of childcare and early years.

Daycare Trust

www.daycaretrust.org.uk

Childcare Hotline 020 78403350

Provides information for parents, childcare providers, employers, trade unions, local authorities and policy makers, on every aspect of childcare.

Ofsted

www.ofsted.gov.uk/parents

Tel: 0845 640 4045 (education, adult skills or local authority children's services)

Tel: 0845 640 4040 (about anything else)

Ofsted inspection reports present a comprehensive and impartial picture of all state funded, and some independant, schools, as well as colleges and teacher training, childminders and day-care. Also the lead inspectorate for reviews of key services for children and young people in each local authority area.

National Childminding Association

www.ncma.org.uk
Tel 0845 880 0044 (Head Office)
NCMA Helpline: 0800 169 4486
The National Childminding Association (NCMA) is the only national charity and membership organisation that speaks on behalf of registered childminders in England and Wales, promoting quality registered childminding so that children, families and communities can benefit from the best in childcare and education.

Sure Start

www.surestart.gov.uk
Public Enquiry Unit on 0870 0002288
Sure Start is the government programme to deliver the best start in life for every child. It brings together early education, childcare, health and family support.

Department for Children, Schools and Families

www.dfes.gov.uk
Tel: 0870 000 2288
Sets out and funds strategies for children's education as well as adult learning.

National Day Nurseries Association

www.ndna.org.uk
Tel: 01484 40 70 70
NDNA is dedicated to the provision, support and promotion of high-quality care and education for the benefit of children, families and communities.

The Pre-school Learning Alliance

www.pre-school.org.uk
Tel: 0207 697 2500
A leading educational charity specialising in the early years, providing practical support to over 15,000 early years settings and making a positive contribution to the care and education of over 800,000 young children and their families each year. They support and actively promote parental involvement in all aspects of their work.

Parents Centre

www.parentscentre.gov.uk

Information and support for parents on how to help with your child's learning, including advice on choosing a school and finding childcare.

Nannytax

www.nannytax.co.uk

Tel. 0845 226 2203

UK payroll service for nannies.

Nanny Care

www.nannyshare.co.uk

If you'd like to have help with the children full or part time, but can't find an affordable way of doing it Nanny Share enables you to get in touch with families in your local area with complementary or similar needs, so that together you can share your childcare.

Employers For Childcare (Northern Ireland)

www.employersforchildcare.org

Employers For Childcare works in partnership with employers, government and childcare providers to promote the business benefits of implementing workplace childcare policies and encouraging businesses to invest in employer-supported childcare.

Small Business Resources

Federation of Small Businesses

www.fsb.org.uk

Tel 01253 336000

The UK's largest organisation lobbying on behalf of and working for small businesses. Vast amounts of info on the site.

The Department of Trade and Industry

www.berr.gov.uk

Tel 020 7215 5000

As well as dealing with consumer and employee issues it seeks to encourage enterprise and innovation and increase productivity in the UK. The Department provides tailored business support as well as advice on grants, loan guarantees and subsidised consultancy. It also has links to lots of other useful government agencies.

Business Link

www.businesslink.gov.uk

Tel. 0845 600 9006

Business Link is an advice, support and information resource provided by the DTI. This site provides practical advice to businesses covering a broad range of topics and links to the relevant government departments. There are also local business link groups across the UK so take a look at the site to find the right one for you. You can also access them through The Chambers of Commerce site (www.chamberonline.co.uk)

HM Revenue and Customs

www.hmrc.gov.uk

This is the official site for HMRC, the department that was Customs and Excise and the Inland Revenue. Here you should be able to find everything you need to know about tax, whether you are a sole-trader or a limited company employing staff as part of your new venture.

Companies House

www.companieshouse.co.uk

Tel. 0870 33 33 636

If you are setting up your own business as a limited company, Companies House is essential for information on how to register and what the implications are for your business. You can also check if that all important company name has already been registered by someone else!

UK Trade and Investment

www.uktradeinvest.gov.uk

Tel +44 (0)20 7215 8000

UK Trade & Investment is the Government organisation that supports UK companies that are doing business internationally, as well as overseas enterprises that are looking to set up or expand in the UK.

J4bgrants

www.j4bgrants.co.uk

If you are looking for funding this is an excellent resource to discover all the UK regional, national and EC grants available. It contains comprehensive information on Government funding for businesses and voluntary groups, as well as a database of publicly funded organisations that provide support and advice.

Information Commissioners Office

www.informationcommissioner.gov.uk

Helpline: 01625 545 745

The Information Commissioners Office can advise you on the Data Protection Act (DPA) and how it may affect your business.

The Office of the e-Envoy

www.cabinetoffice.gov.uk/e-government

The Office of the e-Envoy is part of the Cabinet Office and is better known for the UK Online initiative to get more of the population on the internet, but it is also responsible for promoting electronic business.

HM Revenue & Customs

www.hmrc.gov.uk/startingup/
Guidance on taxation and other duties for start ups and businesses.

Small Business Services

www.sbs.gov.uk.
Tel 0207 215 5000
Advice and information regarding small business.

Professional Organisations and Networking

Everywoman

www.everywoman.co.uk
Tel: 0870 746 1800
Leading provider of valuable, practical and relevant services to support women
in business including a networking forum.

Aurora

www.network.auroravoice.com/home.asp
Aurora identify emerging trends and issues and provide a critical voice to
industry. Aurora's corporate diversity software helps organisations attract,
retain and advance women, thus globally progressing the industry standard.

Changing Direction

www.changingdirection.com
Changing Direction is an organisation dedicated to helping people approach
the workplace after a career break. It is headed by Diana Wolfin, who also
helps those in work, as well as returners, with strategies for a better work-life
balance.

British Association of Women Entrepreneurs

www.bawe-uk.org/
BAWE encourages women to support each other, to enhance recognition of the achievements of women in business and the professions, and promotes the growth of women-owned enterprises through research and sharing information.

Think Pink

www.thinkpinkinc.co.uk
Think Pink Inc is a community driven website, combining a directory with online networking to create a marketplace exclusively tailored to women's needs. It's a great place for customers and businesses to meet.

Business and Professional Woman Network

www.bpwuk.org
Tel: 01246 211 988
BPW UK is an organisation for women, in any type of occupation and at whatever stage of their career development. A non-party-political lobbying organisation, BPW UK gives you the chance to make a difference by influencing policy decisions. In addition, members can receive the encouragement, training and information to apply for public appointments.

Women's Business Network

www.wbn.org.uk/index.php
Tel: 0151 236 6601
This supports the creation of new business networks for women in the North West of England and links these networks together to enable the sharing of good ideas and the expansion of business contacts across the region.

Prowess

www.prowess.org.uk
Prowess is a network of organisations and individuals who support the growth of women's business ownership. Their work encompasses raising awareness, sharing of best practice, advocacy and information.

The Women's Company

www.thewomenscompany.com

Tel: 020 8650 8015

A dynamic membership organisation providing opportunities to UK business women to meet, network and develop business skills with other business women in the UK through local groups. This is achieved by providing quality lunches and events, workshops and seminars which facilitate learning and growth within an organisation.

Parenting

National Council for One Parent Families

www.oneparentfamilies.org.uk

Tel 020 7428 5400, Tel 0800 018 5026 (helpline)

Practical advice, constructive help and consistent support for single parents across a wide range of issues. Incorporates Gingerbread, the leading organisation for lone parent families. A campaigning organisation that also provides a helpline and lots of help and advice from other lone parents.

Contact a Family

www.cafamily.org.uk

Tel 0808 808 3555 (helpline)

Information and support for families caring for children with disabilities.

National Family and Parenting Institute

www.nfpi.org

Tel 020 7424 3460

The National Family and Parenting Institute (NFPI) is an independant charity working to support parents in bringing up their children, to promote the wellbeing of families and to make society more family friendly.

Home-Start

www.home-start.org.uk

Tel 0800 068 63 68

Informal and friendly support for families with young children, provides a lifeline to thousands of parents and children in over 337 communities across the UK and with forces families in Germany and Cyprus. The support is free, confidential and non-judgemental. In fact, almost 25% of families refer themselves to Home-Start - which speaks for itself.

Mumsnet

www.mumsnet.com

A great one stop website for everything a mum could need from product reviews to discounted holidays.

Parentline Plus

www.parentlineplus.org.uk

Freephone: 0808 800 2222

Parentline Plus is a national charity that works for, and with, parents. It offers help and support through an innovative range of free, flexible, responsive services - shaped by parents for parents.

Parentalk

www.parentalk.co.uk

Tel: 020 7921 4234

Parentalk is a national charity dedicated to inspiring and equipping parents to make the most of parenthood.

BBC Parenting

www.bbc.co.uk/parenting

Vast amounts of information, some based on programmes such as Child of Our Time.

Directgov Parents

www.direct.gov.uk/Parents/fs/en

Your legal, financial and employment rights explained as well as advice on applying for benefits etc.

Netmums

www.netmums.com

Local information and support service for parents on childcare, support, activities, schools, friendship and much more.

The Parent Coaching Academy

www.theparentcoachingacademy.com

Leading coaching academy with it's own unique seven day system to help steer you through the problems of parenting as well as tailor made initiatives for employers wishing to help employees.

RaisingKids.co.uk

www.raisingkids.co.uk

As they say themselves, if it's about raising kids, it's on this website! Lots of advice, forums, weekly news, products, tips and shared experiences.

Women and Equality

DTI Women and Equality Unit

www.womenandequalityunit.gov.uk

The Ministers for Women, supported by the Women and Equality Unit (WEU), are responsible for promoting and realising the benefits of diversity in the economy and more widely. Find out what they're doing for you at their website.

The Equality and Human Rights Commission

www.equalityhumanrights.com

The Equality and Human Rights Commission champions equality and human rights for all, working to eliminate discrimination, reduce inequality, protect human rights and to build good relations, ensuring that everyone has a fair chance to participate in society.

Links for Fathers

Fathers Direct

www.fathersdirect.com

The national information centre on fatherhood. They help Government, employers, services for families and children, and families themselves to adapt to changing social roles of men and women. There's loads of advice and information on there, covering a multitude of issues, so if your husband/partner needs a reassuring starting point, then this is it.

For Parents by Parents

www.forparentsbyparents.com/dad.html

Lots of advice, personal experiences and information on everything from finance and legal issues to work issues and personal issues such as post natal depression in men, single fatherhood and changes in relationships after children.

HomeDad.org.uk

www.homedad.org.uk/index.html

Recent research indicates that there are now 200,000 men staying at home to look after the home and family in the UK. And not just house-husbands at home full-time, but increasing numbers of fathers who are working part-time and sharing the childcare, or bringing up children by themselves. A well thought out site that provides plenty of personal information from it's members and takes a big step to demystifying why men might want to stay at home too.

Bibliography

Back to Work: A Guide for Women Returners
Diana Wolfin and Susan Foreman, Robson Books (2004)
The 7 Day Parent Coach
Lorraine Thomas, Vermilion (2005)
Kids & Co.
Ros Jay, White Ladder Press (2003)

Need - 2 - Know

Available Titles

Drugs A Parent's Guide
ISBN 1-86144-043-X £8.99

Dyslexia and Other Learning Difficulties
A Parent's Guide ISBN 1-86144-042-1 £8.99

Bullying A Parent's Guide
ISBN 1-86144-044-8 £8.99

Working Mothers The Essential Guide
ISBN 978-1-86144-048-8 £8.99

Teenage Pregnancy The Essential Guide
ISBN 978-1-86144-046-4 £8.99

How to Pass Exams A Parent's Guide
ISBN 978-1-86144-047-1 £8.99

Child Obesity A Parent's Guide
ISBN 978-1-86144-049-5 £8.99

Sexually Transmitted Infections
The Essential Guide ISBN 978-1-86144-051-8 £8.99

Alcoholism The Family Guide
ISBN 978-1-86144-050-1 £8.99

Divorce and Separation The Essential Guide
ISBN 978-1-86144-053-2 £8.99

Applying to University The Essential Guide
ISBN 978-1-86144-052-5 £8.99

ADHD The Essential Guide
ISBN 978-1-86144-060-0 £8.99

Student Cookbook - Healthy Eating The Essential Guide
ISBN 978-1-86144-061-7 £8.99

Stress The Essential Guide
ISBN 978-1-86144-054-9 £8.99

Single Parents The Essential Guide
ISBN 978-1-86144-055-6 £8.99

Adoption and Fostering A Parent's Guide
ISBN 978-1-86144-056-3 £8.99

Special Educational Needs A Parent's Guide
ISBN 978-1-86144-057-0 £8.99

The Pill An Essential Guide
ISBN 978-1-86144-058-7 £8.99

Diabetes The Essential Guide
ISBN 978-1-86144-059-4 £8.99

To order our titles, please give us a call on **01733 898103**, email **sales@n2kbooks.com**, or visit **www.need2knowbooks.co.uk**

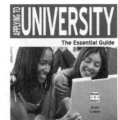
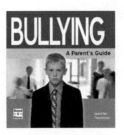

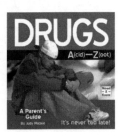

Need - 2 - Know, Remus House, Coltsfoot Drive, Peterborough, PE2 9JX